Gigi Hadid

FLYING HIGH TO SUCCESS, WEIRD AND INTERESTING FACTS ON JELENA NOURA "GIGI" HADID!

Learn all about Gigi Hadid in 20 minutes

With Bern Bolo
The Bathroom Genius

Gigi Hadid

*

*

*

Flying High to Success

*

*

*

Weird and Interesting Facts on
Jelena Noura "Gigi" Hadid!

By Bern Bolo

TABLE OF CONTENTS

***

INTRODUCTION

So hello folks… I am back again and here you are again, reading this entirely new trivia.

Okay, so before anything else, I would like to start this off by saying that this is going to be a new trivia like literally because unlike the ones I have already written from before (*if you have been following my publishes and trivias then you'd know, but if not… it is still fine. It's still never too late to get one now…*)

Woah!!!!!

Okay??? That was very rude and salesy talk right there, right?! LOL.

But anyway, yes… this is going to be, a certainly entirely new trivia because as I've said in the passage above, before I made that salesy and commercially prepared sentences right there…. Unlike the ones I have written before, this one is going to feature not a singer, not a rapper, not a Spanish-speaking macho man, not a boy band member and certainly not Justin Bieber nor Taylor Swift….

I am not meaning something about it… Just saying….

Anyway, so this is a very popular kid who is only 22 years old but has a lifestyle of a 30-year-old successful virgin corporate woman who has worked her ass off to pay the bills for the last 25 years of her life who has now became a millionaire.

That is how fast the life of this young superstar is going today. Autographs here, there and basically everywhere, because she had already been in almost all parts of the freaking globe!

And not to mention the super hot and popular boyfriend with a face full of hair, sexy body tattoos, dreamy eyes, rapper, singer, fashion designer (*because he has his own clothing line now*), model, entrepreneur, actor and of course, to make matters worse… he is of mixed descent, with British and Pakistani parents, seductive and smart accent – what else could you look for?!

I am only pertaining to Zayn Malik guys, the ex-One Direction member….

Yes… the great Zayn Malik and her superstar, supermodel, Model-of-the-year girlfriend – Gigi Hadid.

This is not about Zayn ladies (*if you are a lady reading this trivia…*) this is about **Gigi Hadid**, her lifestyle, her family culture, her ethnicity, we will be including Zayn in some parts of course, about her being part of the volleyball team (*you don't know that do you?*) and about her "Netflix-ing and chilling" with her boyfriend Zayn (*yes and even this…*)

In case you do not know what "Netflix and chill" is…

Then keep on reading through the whole pages of this trivia so you will discover Gigi's almost perfect, luxurious and lavish life and also about "Netflix and chill."

WINK!

BORN "*JELENA NOURA HADID*"

Okay, so without much further blabbering… let us discuss her life, her early beginnings and pretty much anything we can dig and find out about this "IT" gal.

So, Gigi Hadid (as we know her today…) was really born with the biological and true name of Jelena Noura Hadid. Yes, you heard that right – pretty loud and clear actually! This amazing woman is born with a pretty somewhat Arabic name, right?

Well, let me tell you something, not only this sound Arabic *(which the type of name, someone will typically name, on your next-door Arab neighbor…)*, this is a true Arab, actually a true Palestinian name, especially her surname which she got from her dad.

So for you to see the breakdown of her heritage and ethnicity, let's start from the very beginning, shall we?

Okay, so there are two people who fell in love once, one was Palestinian born in Nazareth on November 6, 1948 whose name is Mohamed Anwar Hadid and one was Dutch-American born and raised on Papendrecht, Netherlands who goes by the lovely name of Yolanda van den Herik.

Now, Yolanda here is very much charming, beautiful and undeniably alluring. At an early age, she became a model and traveled to a lot of places including Paris to show off various collections. So Yolanda here fell in love with the then real estate developer Mohamed and got married eventually on 1994.

The couple's blossoming love had been indescribable and priceless. They both had three gorgeous and beautiful children namely, Gigi which was born on April 23, 1995, Bella and Anwar Hadid.

From their marriage and with the added bundles of Joy, Mohamed and Yolanda's relationship together and with their kids had been wonderful, until such time came wherein; things just start to slip away. By early in the year 2000s, the once "happy couple" got divorced, but still, their family image had been constant and is still fine (*good for them…*).

So anyway, though Gigi's parents got divorced, they were still a happy family and even their once small family had become larger, happier and merrier when her mom bore 5 more siblings with her new husband then Mr. David Foster. So all in all, it was still a happy and comfortable life for Gigi.

So while growing up (*even still in under the Hadid household*) Gigi has been displaying random acts of being a supermodel and "*girly*" just like her mom. But nobody has thought that she would even enter the limelight of ramp modeling since back in school at Malibu High School she used to hold the volleyball rather than heels, being prom queen, joining beauty contests or whatnot. She was even the captain of the varsity team, she joined for volleyball and also enjoyed the company of horses – she is a consistent and very good horseback rider.

So if you'd look at it from a normal spectacle – who would imagine that she would be modeling for *Vogue* and *Guess* one day? But here's what did not put into view – *it's in her f*cking blood to be one!* I mean, I believe, I mentioned mom was a super hot model back in her days right? So it is inevitable for her to follow the same steps.

According to a source, it started as a type-of-a-hobby for her once, but when Gigi started to gain popularity and of course good money with modeling, she just kinda went for it and continued to be one – *and boy… she was good!*

Awesome work on that one Gigi!

SHE'S NOT NEW TO SHOW BUSINESS: THE ICONIC PARENTS

So, as I have already talked about in the pages before this, Gigi has been living the life ever since she was younger.

I mean c'mon… being the child of two successful and prominent folks… what else you could ask for?!

Well… she could have asked for more ice cream when she was a kid, and a very expensive dress for prom night when she was in high school right???

Any who! My point is, she had a wonderful life, though her parents signed the divorce papers but still she grew up filled with love and passion in her heart. She became a model at a young age, she was horseback riding and she was doing volleyball! All thanks to her amazing parents who have played a big role in molding her future in the industry.

As I have stated in the earlier pages, Gigi had been living the popular life since. Her mother Yolanda Hadid former Yolanda van den Herik was a model and TV personality. She "starred" in the reality TV show named The Real Housewives of Beverly Hills – pretty familiar right? Well, that's because it is just one of the most successful and most-watched TV series in America. That's why it sounds familiar. Mother Yolanda here, was born in the Netherlands with one brother named Leo. Her mom, (*basically Gigi's grandmother*) raised Yolanda and her Leo all by herself since her husband (*Yolanda's dad and Gigi's grandfather*) died in a car accident.

Like Gigi, while growing up, she displayed amazing beauty and grace until a Dutch designer through the name of Frans Molenaar had discovered her and made her a model in one of his shows which then later had been discovered with another model producer named Eileen Ford which made Yolanda a part of her circle of models group named "Ford Models."

Since then, Yolanda's modeling career blossomed until she hit 15 years in the modeling field where she decided to settle down with the then, real-estate developer – Mohamed Hadid who is also quite well-known for his amazing talents in the said field.

By that time, Mohamed is already popular and had already established quite a name for himself.

He was born Jordanian-American who has Palestinian origin. And actually, Gigi's dad is not only famous for the buildings he built and the luxurious mansions he designed, he is also famous for being a descendant of an Arab royalty. Though Mohamed hasn't stated that he is purely into the Muslim religion but still character shows when he doesn't even drink his 5,000 bottles of premium wine in his wine cellar!

And of course, if you have a king for a great, great, great grandfather – *then you should be asking for servants to open those damn wines!*

So anyway, the two met and there had been an instant spark. And right after a number of months of dating, they decided to tie the knot eventually.

And though they have separated their ways already, the two are still identified "powerful" while coupling with other dominating names in the Hollywood industry like for Gigi's mom – she married producer David Foster afterwards and her dad Mohamed became engaged to a businesswoman and a model named Shiva Safai whom he proposed to back in 2014.

So see? Told you Gigi had always been close to show business…

GROWING UP DUTCH-PALESTINIAN & A ROYALTY DESCENDANT?

Okay…. So I have been wanting to tackle this topic since the beginning of this trivia. Because I have been repeating it over and over again on most of the pages about the mix ethnicities Gigi and her family has.

So, let me get something straight right here… I'm going to try and race Gigi's family tree alright?

So, her mother is half Dutch, half American and her father is half Jordanian, half Palestinian and is half American, so in short… *because I know you might be raising your eyebrows right now….*

In short, Gigi is part Dutch, part Jordanian, part Palestinian and American all at the same time.

Okay! Even more confusing! LOL.

Anyway, let's just have it like this, she is Dutch-Palestinian with a royal blood. So okay, is that easier now?

Okay great…

So, growing up in a mixed-ethnicity household is really not that much of a big deal especially for Gigi.

I mean, the Hadid family has certainly been doing great. One day they pray while doing the sign of the cross, the next day, they could be praising and worshiping Allah, or

the next day they'd be Christians, or Muslims or by the next day they wanted to touch more on the Palestinian culture or maybe the Dutch one…

But either way, whether Dutch, Palestinian, Jordanian or American…. The important thing is each of them understands one another in their family.

It is actually better knowing that Gigi had got her "girly", charming and sweet side more on her mom and her somewhat "boyish" traits sometimes – like loving volleyball and horseback riding and being fierce from her dad.

And of course, let's us not forget about her having the royal blood whom she had acquired from her father's side.

But anyway, as confusing as her race may get, Gigi made the best out of her Life.

She just definitely showcased to all people in all parts of the globe on how flexible and versatile she can be.

And not to mention, the reason behind she is now considered one of the *Queens of the Catwalk*...

EXPLAINING THE 'ROYAL BLOOD' OF THE

CATWALK'S QUEEN

Okay, Gigi… so you have a royal blood?

That means you are just more fitting to own that Catwalk ramp right? You're even labeled, literally, as for today's generation's Catwalk queen!

Well, let's blame it on her blood first! Because...basically, Mohamed, Gigi's dad is Palestinian as I told you about. Though, he was part Jordanian and American, but his origin came from the land of every Christian's savior and God Jesus Christ which is Nazareth.

Yes, Gigi's daddy is from Nazareth, but when I said that her family and his dad's family are the descendants of the royal blood – let me clear one thing… I am certainly not pertaining to Jesus okay (*as we have all been told...*) I am pertaining to the recent Kings that came after.

So Gigi's dad is the son of Anwar Hadid and wife Khairiah. Through Khairiah, Gigi's grandmommy in her father's side, Mohamed had gotten his royal genes and DNA. His mom is the great, great, great, great-granddaughter of the former ruler and leader of the northern part of the Palestine empire named Zahir al-Umar al-Zaydani or known better as Daher Al Omer.

For those of you who doesn't know who is the great Daher Al Omer of Palestine… he is just the one who had successfully beat and has withstood threats and assaults from the then Ottoman empire and its greedy governors who wanted him out from his prestigious position.

The place was awesome and nice back then when king Daher ruled the land. It was peaceful and quiet. Though there are certainly some rules everyone needs to follow, the goal there is to achieve organization and prosperity.

And because of this, he finally became famous to the people there and this had influenced his Sheikhdom eventually. And to finance his title, he used and controlled the trading of both olive oil and cotton goods to Europe.

It was actually a smart and wise way to control the flow of money while joining forces and making allies with other countries to promote the betterment of life and his people.

Now, in an overall point of view… King Daher has been a good ruler and a wise one. He had promoted safety and equality in all his fellowmen. He was a great example indeed!

And so behold the fruit of his blood in this generation – Gigi Hadid who has been outstanding in her endeavors and passions in life.

Gigi is at heart a kind and loving person, but like her great grandpapa, when it comes to rules and fierceness, she had definitely shown it all, well not by ruling in the Palestinian villages of course, but by ruling the Catwalk!

She's definitely a 'queen' in her time – *she's the queen of the Catwalk!*

GIVING UP CRIMINAL PSYCHOLOGY TO STUDY HEELS, MAKEUP & LIPSTICK!

So, that was a nice story, isn't it? So, we have already learned about her parents, her childhood and even about the story of her highness…

So now, we will be moving forward to another timeline in her life, just right before she completely entered the modeling scene.

Now, it is vitally important for me to state this one out, because I have to be clear with you, just like I said in some passages and pages from this trivia, I said that this girl is definitely not like your typical teenage girl while growing up, I mean she wanted to stand out and she wanted to be different! In a very good way though…

So anyway, other girls while growing up wanted to go on a lot of dates, change boyfriends every now and then like how often they change their clothes and worry about their hair, worry about the sun hitting their skin and even worrying about dirt – yes it's normally true that some girls, the teenage ones most specifically are very vain, but our star right here is certainly not like that.

She played volleyball while growing up, she do horseback ridings – *nope, definitely not scared of dirt at all and the sun hitting her precious skin, oh no, no, no….*

And to make her life even more interesting, she studied a peculiar course when she was in college (*well at least odd for some…*) she studied freaking Criminal Psychology at The New School back in Manhattan!

So do you even know what this means? Well this means that she wanted to study a criminal's mind, behavior, traits and their mentality.

Oh well, that is one hell of a brave gal right there!

Oh yes, she is, but you see guys… at the end of the day, she still settled on her feminine side and by late 2013, Gigi who's supposed to be the future Criminal Psychologist, who's gonna be in every criminal's dream of having in an interview room decided to follow her mom's path and sealed her fate when she dropped the study to focus on some modeling career.

And that is exactly how she dropped being a psychologist to focus more on the girly stuff!

Way to go Gigi girl!!!

THE GLAMOROUS LIFE OF GIGI HADID

Okay, so right then and there, after she dropped the bomb that she wasn't going to study Criminal Psychology anymore, she then dropped another career bomb – when she went straight to New York after dropping her school to be a model in a professional way, this time. So eventually, Gigi has made this, her career. She went and signed a contract with IMG models in New York city back in 2013 and made her first appearance as an adult in New York runway for the New York Fashion week on February of 2014.

But here's some few fun facts, before she professionally signed with IMG, she already appeared as a guest model for various well-known clothing brands and lines like Guess. Unfortunately, by this time she had to focused on her studies, so she stopped for a while and just made it a part-time gig. So anyway, being in the IMG models circle has been a great start for Gigi. After her consistent run shows, she was later contacted on few more prestigious acts for few more prestigious brands and covers.

She made it on the cover of CR Fashion Book Magazine on July 2014, modeling along with the Hollywood superstar and model Patrick Schwarzenegger for the designer Tom Ford. And she had also appeared in the cover of Galore Magazine. And yes, life was certainly doing great for Gigi – and it even offered her more! As she had been invited by Vogue for their cover and also had become a Maybelline brand Ambassador!

And here's more… she also modeled for Tommy Hilfiger, Victoria's Secret, Versace, The CR Fashion Book, Vogue US, LOVE Magazine and more!

Oh yes… she totally made a very good career and living out from that rocking body right?!

Totally the glamorous life of being a model eh….

GIGI & ZAYN MALIK GOES STEAMY (*LIKE ALL THE F*CKING TIME*) WITH "*NETFLIX & CHILL*"

Ahermmmm…. Ahermmm…. Ahermmm…

(*Continues to cough until the last page…*)

(*Just kidding – didn't want you to think I have a horrible disease or something…*)

So anyway, I just want to clear out some air, because this topic is going to be quite the "*parental-guidance-is-needed*" type.

This is going to be a very sensitive topic so I want you guys to know that I'm gonna be very subtle and slow here, alright?

Okay…

So this topic is all about Gigi and Zayn Malik's SEX life.

Whew!!! I hope that was slow enough for you guys! That was a hard one right there!

So anyway, yes… you heard and read that right, this is all going to be about these two lovebird's sex life as described by Gigi's boyfriend Zayn Malik – the former One Direction member.

Okay so, as for Zayn, sex is very important to them both and they actually do the "Netflix and Chill" (*which means sex by the way*) EVERY F*CKING SINGLE DAY…

Well, who could blame Zayn, right? I mean, you have a very hot model as a girlfriend and him being a very hot boyfriend, who could resist who! And the two is living together in Zayn's mansion in Los Angeles – what could possibly go wrong right?!

REFERENCES

https://en.wikipedia.org/wiki/Gigi_Hadid

https://en.wikipedia.org/wiki/Mohamed_Hadid

https://en.wikipedia.org/wiki/Yolanda_Hadid

https://en.wikipedia.org/wiki/Zahir_al-Umar

http://stylecaster.com/zayn-malik-gigi-hadid-sex/

http://metro.co.uk/2017/03/15/zayn-malik-and-gigi-hadid-are-sickly-sweet-in-interview-with-versace-6510746/

https://en.wikipedia.org/wiki/IMG_Models

https://web.archive.org/web/20150801202931/http://www.yolanda.com/about/my-family

http://www.eonline.com/news/475761/real-housewives-of-beverly-hills-star-yolanda-foster-s-daughter-gigi-hadid-models-for-guess-see-the-pretty-pic

http://www.vogue.co.uk/article/vogue-arabia-gigi-hadid-cover

http://digital.modernluxury.com/article/The+Radar+People/453793/0/article.html

http://www.imgmodels.com/new-york/women/model/portfolio?mid=9161

http://www.glammonitor.com/2014/09/18/gigi-hadid-opens-eyes/

http://www.glamourmagazine.co.uk/gallery/zayn-malik-and-gigi-hadid-dading-and-relationship-news

http://socawlege.com/9-beautiful-girls-zayn-malik-has-dated/2/

https://www.instagram.com/gigihadid/?hl=en

https://www.facebook.com/officialgigihadid/

https://twitter.com/GiGiHadid?ref_src=twsrc%5Egoogle%7Ctwcamp%5Eserp%7Ctwgr%5Eauthor

Check Out CNCO "Our La Banda Winners" Trivia!

Guys have heard about the Latin Reggaeton music genre? Well, if your Spanish or just a fan, I'm pretty sure you may have heard this one. But if you have not, then you came to the right place – I mean trivia… (*or just place to make it more commonly clear…*) so if you want to know more about Spanish Reggaeton and the Latin music scene and even how English producer Simon Cowell have come to create a Latin-American show, then click that little button now and grab one! Not only you will learn about a few world cultures, but most especially about the pop group CNCO! So get one and grab some for your friends too!

Check Out CNCO's Trivia
[Get your copy of CNCO's Trivia!](#)

If you enjoyed this "Trivia", please leave an honest review on Amazon.com!

Sign-up here on [Bern Bolo's](#) site for Trivia On Twenty One Pilots!